Dead Friends in New Mexico

Missing You

Helen M. Walters

BookLeaf
Publishing
India | USA | UK

Dedication

This book is dedicated to my husband, Frederick Edward Walters Jr. aka FEW. We met through our poetry and art. Collaborating on poems and art for 32 years, we had quite an adventure. Meeting in Philadelphia, living n New Jersey and New Mexico, moving back and forth across the country and finally settling down in Roswell, NM for his retirement.

He was diagnosed with chronic PTSD from his time in the service of the US Marine Corps. He was treated in the VA health system. He was an artist who created up until the month he passed away, I am lucky to have not just the memories of our time together, but all his poems and artwork as well.

Before he left the planet, he said to me, "I lived in Taos, Albuquerque and Roswell, but I never got to live in Santa Fe, so make sure I am buried in the National Cemetery. I'll retire there." And that is where he rests in peace, whole again in mind and body, on a hill overlooking the scenery of Santa Fe.

Acknowledgement

I would like to thank my poetry group, the High Prairie Poets Society of Roswell, NM for keeping me active in the poetry world. I am grateful for the "Open Mic" nights at Stellar's Coffee on Main Street and the Black Cock Brewery on Southeast Main Street in Roswell, where I share my written words. I am thankful for the two Brankas who asked 9 poets from our Roswell community to submit their works that were published in Macedonia. Thank you Senior Circle for allowing me to share poetry with the seniors there. I want to thank my family and friends for supporting me in my writing efforts, those who came to the open mic nights, and those people whom I have inspired to write their own poetry.

Preface

I've lived in many places in New Mexico and had many friends. Each relationship left an indelible memory. I have captured them here in the form of poetry. As I age, I send less mail at Christmas and I cross off names in my address book. So I start my journey with those people and share their stories.

Missing Him

He would use funny voices
and make funny faces,
and use a lot of hand gestures
when he told a story.

He commanded the full attention of the
room,
or he'd start the whole story over.

He said "don't cry for me."
So at home, I try not to.
It's when I try to talk to people
about his passing.

When accepting condolences,
That's when I choke up and tears well up.
And I do my best not to break down
and there I push it inside.

Yes, I am missing him every day,
always in a different way.
 I'm missing him, can I just say,
I am missing him in every way.

Mr. Robert Reynolds

Robert was the group leader for many, many
years.
His poems would bring us insight,
 joy and sometimes a few tears.
He'd thank us for being here
 and then he'd always say,
"This poetry club would not be here,
 if we did not come out today."

We'd go around the table
and each had a poem to read.
Each held a piece of paper
 with words waiting to be freed.
And as we read each poem aloud,
 we shared the spoken word.
The audience would listen, with attention
to everything they heard.

Sometimes we'd hear the story
of what made them write this poem.
It might be a life experience,
or memory of a childhood home.
Robert was a volunteer, and always a Marine.

He loved to sing a solo hymn,
at many churches, he was seen.

And Robert was a man of God,
he really loved the Lord.
And he had a loving wife in Dawn,
who Robert long adored.
Tom is Robert's long-time friend
who was always by his side.
Together, they did everything.
Between them, nothing to hide.

His family, Dawn, Tom and so many people in
town,
Whose lives he touched, who knew him well,
are now all feeling down.
What more can we say about him, now he's
gone.
We'll remember how he served and loved
and wrote and sang his song.

A Vanished Friend

Around the corner I have a friend,
In this great state that has no end.
Yet the days go by and weeks rush on
and before I know it, a year has gone.

And I never see my old friend's face,
for life is a swift and terrible race.
He knows I like him just as well
as in the days when I rang his bell.

And he rang mine, but we were younger then,
and now we are busy tired men.
Tired of playing a foolish game,
tired of trying to make a name.

"Tomorrow" I say, "I will call on Tim"
just to show that I'm thinking of him.
But tomorrow comes and tomorrow goes,
and the distance between us grows and grows.

Around the corner, yet miles away,
"Here's a message sir, Tim died today."

And that's what we get and deserve in the
end.
Around the corner, a vanished friend.

Where Angels Go to Cry
The Legend of the Sangre de Christo Mountains

It's way up there in the sky.
That's how angels stay so high,
They're so much nearer to the sky,
and under God's watchful eye.

And when good humans die,
the angels sob and sigh
and head up to the mountains
where angels go to cry.

When angels go to cry
they'll stay up all night
and contemplate in rhyme
while tears fall from the sky.
and drop on mountains high,
where angels go to cry.

I never knew about them
until my husband dear,
said let's go to New Mexico!
And that's how I got here.

I never thought I'd leave them
but left them for a year.
But grieve I did and so I'm back
to share with them my tears.

It's really been a healing
to come back here and cry.
Although I'm not an angel,
I am closer to the sky.

Mist

I drove through a cloud today.
A cloud sitting on the earth.
A bone chilling, damp fog.
The cloud wraps around trees and houses.
And my car.
It sits on a lake or a river.
It grounds the birds, they sit and swim.
I crossed the river
where the clouds come to drink.
And as it sucks the drops heavenward
some fell, but just a few,
and they landed on my windshield,
the glass that protects me
from a crying cloud.

I looked out the front door
early one morning after he died.
A dark shape was at the end of the porch
wavering in the mist
and as the sun came up
it disappeared into the lingering water
droplets

of the cloud being erased
by the light of day.

Ode to Carrie

She died like Jimmy Dean.
I visited the place she died.
I asked her spirit to speak to mine.
I felt her walk through me.
in the shadow of that wall.
I walked across the grass,
and felt her spirit call.

I gazed upon the scene
of where she met her maker.
Death brought on by a man she loved,
who in the end would forsake her.

Her neck was broke on impact
and she died like Jimmy Dean.
Revived again by the EMT's
She died a second time at the scene.

A Simple Fishtown service
with 300 people there,
A simple Fishtown girl
who never went anywhere.
But now she's gone,

no taxes will she pay.
I never pictured her as one
who'd age with hair of gray.

So maybe it was a blessing for
the girl with tats and pierced tongue,
who I don't think was all that bad,
cause only the good die young.

Sammy Salcido

We had a neighbor, who was a quiet man.
He was our age, but blind was Sam.
He loved to sit outside in the sun,
He's smile and talk to anyone.
You's see him talking on his phone
sitting in front of his humble home.
He lived with his dog and several birds
and "Bubba" listened to all his words.
Never lonely, though he lived alone
You often find him on the phone.
Church friends would take him out for a ride.
and when he heard my husband outside,
He'd call out, "Is that you Fred?"
"Let's have a chat before I go to bed."
Sam never married or had a kid,
He prayed to God, that's what he did.
Glaucoma took his sight away,
slowly, cruelly, day by day.
He broke his leg one day when he fell
and life became a living hell.
Away from home for a long time,
Fred made sure birds and Bubba were fine.
Sam finally made the journey home

We checked on him, still being alone.
Someone came in 3 times a week,
but that caregiver wouldn't speak
She wouldn't give him the time of day
or let him know the weather today
Sam had a cousin in Midland
who would come by to lend a hand.
And when Sam died,
she's the one who cried.
She was his close friend for life,
cause Sam never took a wife.
Everything was such a blur
but she called Fred, his neighbor,
and told him he was like a brother
and gave him Sam's stuff, it was for no other.
So I think of Sam most every day
as I move his knick knacks out of the way.
I miss my neighbor, the quiet man
friend forever, our brother Sam.

Missing a Sister

Never again will you meet - a woman so
sweet.
She was stubborn and strong,
she lived well and long.
But for us, you see, she died all too soon,
never again to see stars and the moon.
She really loved her family,
her son, daughters and grand babies.

She'd always go the extra mile
to do things for them to make them smile.
They are really, really going to miss
the way she'd greet them, hug and kiss.

We will miss this woman, but remember her
life.
We'll never know about her times of strife.
She hid them well with her laugh and smile...
And everything she did, she did in style.
She kept her family together, all four kids
She worked extra hard, that's what she did.

She loved to vacation with them to many
places
and put big smiles on all their faces.

So don't you weep, don't you cry
She's only on the other side.
And we carry her memories as we go,
'cause we loved her more than you'll ever
know.
I'm going to miss you sister dear,
and so will all the others gathered here.
You'll always be with me, in my heart,
so we will never really be apart.

My Mama

She suffered in silence, all of those years,
Not letting anyone see her tears.
If you came to visit, she'd put on her face
and talk and she'd smile with all of her grace.

But when she was alone again,
the blood and tears would flow then
and she'd say to herself - "When I am 65,
I'll get a check up - if I'm still alive."

But she only made it to 63,
cause one night she fell down on her knee
and she couldn't get up, she had broken a hip.
In the darkness of night - she let a cry slip.

"Oh God, why'd you let this happen to me?
I tried to be strong, so no one would see,
or know of this ailment I have deep inside."
She couldn't get up, so she lay there and cried.

They came to her aid, eight men - all strong.

But in her despair, she knew something was
wrong.
She's crying and feels blood rushing again,
but this time, it all went right to her brain.

One ailment had swiftly turned into more.
She died, 3 days short of turning sixty-four.
But no more will she suffer in a body so ill,
Nothing could save her, no doctor, no pill.

So when I get to see her again,
I know it will be up there in heaven.
She'll not be in pain, she'll once again be
whole.
God knows she had suffered, but she's still a
good soul.

We Died

I had to change my name - don't you see,
for when they buried my mother,
they also buried me.

To see your name on a headstone -
To see the date that she died -
To feel that something's missing,
ripped out from inside.

You've given me an identity
by calling me Helen-Marie,
I am who I was again.
Reflective, loving, caring
I am able to be sharing
my life and be my own best friend.

A Rich Man's Death

My father died a rich man's death,
that's what he got with his last breath.
I spoke to him just the night before,
not knowing that - he was at death's door.

When I found out, I wept and I cried.
At home, in his sleep, my father had died.
He lay down on the couch to watch some TV,
right after talking on the phone with me.

With teeth in his mouth, and his glasses still
on
smiling at a show where a contestant had
won.
He closed his eyes just to rest them a bit.
And that's when the old ticker inside of him
quit.

He was so full of wisdom, so alive!
But he was gone in 4 hours, maybe five.
I had no warning his life would end,
and that I would be losing a really good
friend.

I thought," How could death have grabbed
him that way?
But that's what he wanted - so he would say..
To die at home and in you sleep,
Sons and daughters - don't you weep.

A Friend's Friend

There was a woman who worked for a friend,
she was often ill, and would think it was the
end.
And she worked so very hard
when she was cleaning up the yard.
She would pull out every weed,
pick up pecans and rake elm seed.

She cleaned hotels and houses too.
Going home so tired and feeling blue.
But she would get up another day,
and with her family she would play.

Yes, we will miss her very much.
Her smile, her friendship and loving touch.
She has no more burdens and is out of pain,
but we will remember her, happy again.

Losing her left a hole in our hearts,
in our memories we go back to the start.
Remembering the good and bad times she
had.
She worked through it all, then later feel glad.

She was sweet and kind, never mean.
We will always remember our sweet Pauline.
23

Dana

Dana owned a contemporary gallery
bringing New York art for all to see.
Holding openings for all the shows
receptions for all the buyers she knows.

She needed a manager for her parking lot
and an honest man was what she got.
Collecting just two dollars a day
from tourists who would come and stay
and visit the plaza and all the stores.
Monthly spaces paid a bit more.

And so we became a part of her crowd
who gathered as friends, conversing quite
loud.
Intellectuals who had traveled the world,
and Jasper the cat, in the corner he curled.

We moved away, but kept in touch
and then we didn't hear too much.
The gallery was closed and she got divorced.
She didn't want to, she was forced.

She worked for her lawyer and then passed
the bar,
moved to Hawaii, in our eyes, a star!
But then she got cancer, becoming quite sick,
went to California where she would pick,

To be with her brother to spend her last
breath,
and later we would hear about her death.
She came in a dream to my husband, her
friend
I googled her name and found in the end,

all these details of her life, but the cancer had
won.
We'll remember all those days in the sun.
A cute, petite blond with a drink in her hand
We lost a sister in this enchanted land.

John Brown

My husband worked with a man in town
who went by the name of John Brown.
A music promoter in earlier days
now selling cars to those who would pay.

He also worked at the Adobe Press
a newspaper that was such a mess
It once had a staff of sixteen
Now there was only five on the scene.

John would start a secret affair
with a business woman in Taos where
they would meet in the back of her gallery
in the quiet of night, so no one could see.

Their love was strong and grew and grew,
and before long the whole town knew
Her divorce left her without anything,
but they stayed together, he gave her a ring.

She took care of him through to the very end
of his life and were the best of friends.
She took his ashes on one last balloon ride

scattering them across the countryside.

27

Phone Buddies

Although my older sister passed away six
years ago.
Her husband lived on so sad, you know.
And as my other sister on hospice, was dying,
I'd send cards and notes, really trying
to perk her up and show some love.
I thought I heard a voice from above
and decided my brother-in-law needed a card
so I wrote of memories, it wasn't that hard.
And when he got it, I triggered a chain
of notes and phone calls, cause he would
claim
that he wasn't very good with a pen,
but I learned it was often that way with men.

And so I looked forward to getting his call
and he eagerly waited to hear it all.
I'd tell him what things I'd done that week.
We'd talk and laugh till he just couldn't speak.
He'd tire, get winded and have to sign off
and sometimes laugh so hard that he'd cough.

I kept sending cards, he loved getting mail.
We spoke of our youth, he'd tell me a tale
of growing up in the south down Florida way
so clear and detailed like it happened today.

And we'd both reminisce
about people we missed
Then hang up the phone
to be left all alone.
His condition got worse and calls became less.
I knew his condition would never regress.
Then one day I got a call from my niece,
that this man we both loved, was now at
peace

The Collector

My husband met Bruce while I was working
And helped sort his stuff, there was this and
that thing.
Bruce had been sick, pancreatic cancer
diagnosis.
The men talked a lot. Fred said, "You'll get
through this."

Their friendship was short, the cancer soon
spread.
And we got a call that his friend Bruce was
dead.
The brother came up from Texas way,
With so much to handle, they just had to stay.

And we helped them to sort out all of the
stuff,
three houses in all, it really was rough.

They decided since such a friend, Fred had
been

and Bruce talked about him right up to the
end,
To give to Fred all the things that were left.
So much to be dealt with, after a death.

And Bruce will be remembered for the rest of
all times,
when I use things that were his, and now they
are mine.

Pagan Girl

When we first met at her shop
Earthway Herbs, it was called.
There was a ton of knowledge
behind that door and walls.

She made quite an impression on my husband
and I.
She had shelves of jars - herbs, hand-picked
and dried.

We moved away and out of state
with some of her products, they were top rate.
We thought of her often but fell out of touch.
our lives took priority and we didn't think of
her much.

But we came back here to live, and then
looked her up
She made medicine bags now, like a small
leather cup.

We had a few visits, good times as old friends,

The visits were short for her life would soon
end.
Lung cancer would take her from this world
a down home, southern, pagan girl.

The Farmer's Friend

Jim Gill was a hero to many.
Without him, there's be no crops a plenty.
Owner of a store called Roswell Seed,
he had solutions for those in need.
When something went wrong out in the field,
He'd get you the answer to bring up your
yield.
And when you were the right kind of
shopper,
He'd set right down and tell you a whopper.
Geraniums and tomato plants
Fertilizer and farmer's pants.
He took care of the garden show,
grew giant pumpkins too, you know.
And when he finally passed,
It was for Roswell, the saddest day.
At his service, the crowds did show
and we could still hear him on the radio.
And though farmers all over are sad,
we can now hear the latest ad
And still listen as if the phrase was new

just ask yourself, "What would Jim Gill do?

35

Memories

There are so many people I knew in this state,
They were a part of my life, oh
it was great to have met them and make
memories
to share with you now, if you please.

We lived in three places,
there are so many faces
that will pop up in my head
a memory of people, who are dead.

I remember them fondly, I'll look up and
smile,
cause some I knew for a very short while.
And I don't know if they remembered me,
What matters, is they each had a story.

NOTE:
Up in Taos,we lost Tom, Rusty, Roger, Dana,
and John.
In Roswell, Lucille, Bruce, Charles, Sam, Kat,

Pauline, Joanne, Jim, Luther, Barbara, Robert
and Dawn,
and my husband Fred.

Descansos

Little altars found along the roadsides,
left to remember those who have died.
Crosses, flowers, candles, teddy bears,
that last one always brings me to tears.
They are up and down main street,
where someone was hit, knocked off their
feet.

To find out what happened I look to the
news,
the internet, TV, radio, looking for clues.
Was it a head on? or a single car?
Does anyone know how many there are?
A dust storm where mom died and daughter
survived.
How many died? How many cried?

The Honey Man

He had his spot for twenty years
 at the farm and growers market under the
same tree.
It was along fourth street off of Main where
he
sold his produce, plants figs and specialty -
honey.
As the years went by he grew a following
that would visit and by from him every year.
And as time went on, his health would
decline,
but he would show up, not shedding a tear.
He had many helpers to bring out his many
wares
and set up his tent and tables.
He'd sit there with his little dog,
with his oxygen tubes, doing what he was
able.
He loved to talk to customers, friends and
strangers,
with many stories to tell.
Some days there were more stories and
talking done,

then having things to sell.
We'll miss our Luther dearly,
but we know his Lord had another plan.
So in our heart we'll keep the memory of
the grower's market fig and honey man.